Border Breakdown

THE FALL OF THE BERLIN WALL

SMITHSONIAN INSTITUTION

For my parents, Tommy, and our remarkable girls Katie and Maddie—M.M.S.

Book copyright © 2011 Palm Publishing, LLC, 353 Main Avenue, Norwalk, CT 06851, and the Smithsonian Institution, Washington, DC 20560.

Published by Soundprints, an imprint of Palm Publishing, LLC, Norwalk, Connecticut.
www.soundprints.com

Editors: Barbie Heit Schwaeber and Tracee Williams
Book design: Katie Sears
Audio design: Barbie Heit Schwaeber
Production coordinator: Chris Dobias

First Edition 2011
10 9 8 7 6 5 4 3 2 1
Printed in China

Acknowledgements:
    Our very special thanks to Jennifer Locke Jones, Chair and curator of the Division of Armed Forces History at the Smithsonian Institution for her review of this book.
    Our very special thanks to Ellen Nanney and Kealy Wilson at the Smithsonian Institution's Office of Product Development and Licensing for their help in the creation of this book.

Library of Congress Cataloging-in-Publication Data is on file with the publisher and the Library of Congress.

Border Breakdown

THE FALL OF THE BERLIN WALL

by Molly Smith
Illustrated by David Opie

"Lucy is late," Kevin says to his friends, Tomas and Emma. They are waiting in *The Price of Freedom* exhibit at the National Museum of American History.

"I'm right here!" Lucy gasps as she runs toward the group. "That cross-town bus is such a hassle. Sometimes I feel like it's impossible to get around in this city."

"At least you are allowed to get around the city. Hey, check this out," says Kevin, pointing to a case holding three pieces of concrete in the Cold War section of the exhibit.

"Those just look like chunks of concrete," says Tomas. "They even have some graffiti on them."

"These are pieces of the Berlin Wall from Germany," says Kevin.

"After World War II, Germany was divided into sections," Lucy adds. "West Berlin was run by Europe and the United States. East Berlin was run by the Soviet Union. Many people in East Berlin did not want to be taken over by the Communist government of the Soviet Union, so they started fleeing to West Berlin."

"So the government actually built a wall to keep people from leaving?" Tomas asks in disbelief.

"That's right," says Lucy. "People woke up one morning and found out they couldn't leave their part of the city."

"Can you imagine if there was a wall dividing Washington, D.C.?" asks Emma. "What if we were separated on opposite sides of it? We wouldn't be able to see each other."

Lucy shivers at the thought. It would be awful if she couldn't see her best friends again.

"It's really hard to believe something like that could happen," Lucy says as she stares at the concrete.

Suddenly, Lucy hears an unfamiliar voice and feels a tap on her shoulder. "Liesel! Are you listening to me?"

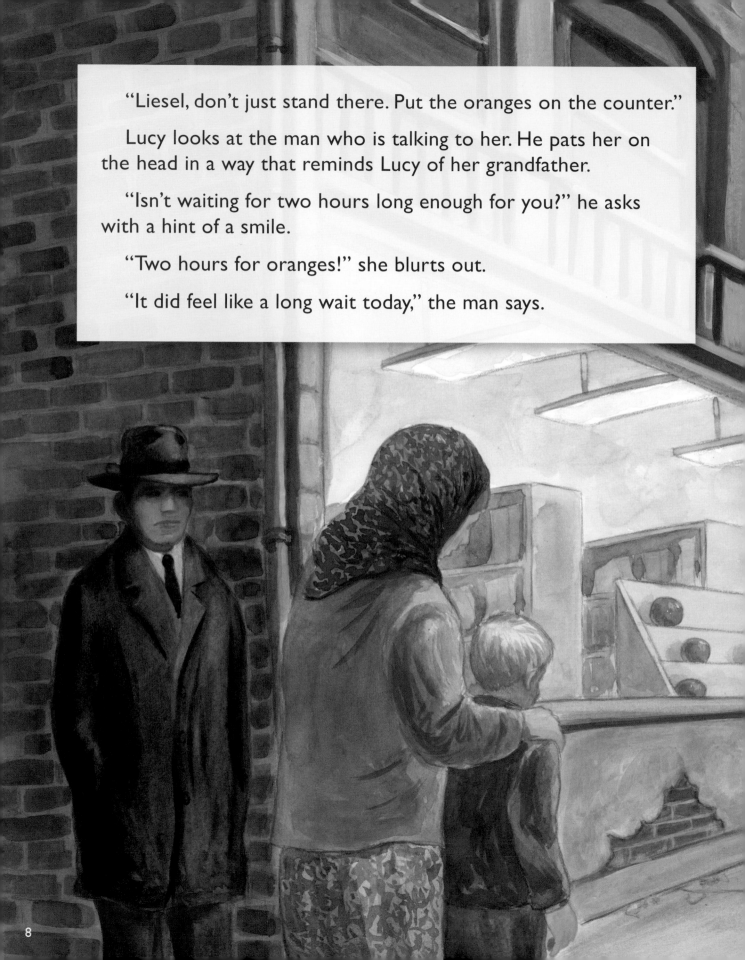

"Liesel, don't just stand there. Put the oranges on the counter."

Lucy looks at the man who is talking to her. He pats her on the head in a way that reminds Lucy of her grandfather.

"Isn't waiting for two hours long enough for you?" he asks with a hint of a smile.

"Two hours for oranges!" she blurts out.

"It did feel like a long wait today," the man says.

What kind of place is this? she thinks, looking around at the half-empty shelves. All the products look old, yet people seem desperate to buy them. The man pays, holds out his hand, and says, "Stick close to your Opa today, Liesel. There's been a lot of trouble."

This man thinks I'm his granddaughter, Liesel, Lucy realizes. She follows him down a street lined with big, cement buildings. People hurry by with their heads down and a man in a dark suit lurks at the corner. Smoke puffs out of factories nearby. The air smells strange and the sky is gray.

Lucy and Opa arrive at a large apartment building where the Kruger family lives. They walk quickly up to an apartment on the second floor.

"We're home," calls Opa.

As the family members come into the kitchen, Lucy looks out the back window. She sees a huge concrete wall topped with barbed wire. To her right, she sees a watchtower with two men standing stifly, holding guns. One of the guards catches Lucy's eye and raises his gun slightly.

She whips around. That's when she sees a calendar that reads, November 1989. "That's the Berlin Wall," she whispers. Looking around the old-fashioned apartment she thinks, *I must be in East Berlin!*

"Were you followed by the secret police again today, Opa?" asks a woman who must be Liesel's mother.

"I don't think so," Opa says.

"Who was that man by the grocery store?" Lucy asks.

"I don't know, Liesel," says Opa. "We can't be sure of anything. Since your Uncle Kurt and his family escaped, the Stasi will be watching our every move."

"I understand why Kurt and his family left," says Oma. "But it still breaks my heart. The Wall is a terrible thing, but at least all of us were on the same side. What if I never see my son again?"

"This wouldn't be happening if the government didn't cage us in," says a boy a little older than Lucy. "That's why people are trying to escape. A government that has to keep its people in with a wall is doomed to fail."

"Hans!" Opa says in a sharp, but low voice. "You can be put in jail for criticizing the government. Our apartment could have microphones—the Stasi may be listening."

"I know, Opa," says Hans. "I'm just tired of feeling scared all the time. I should be able to say whatever I want. I'm not saying I want to escape to the West, but I should be free to visit if I wish!"

"How can the government tell people what to say and think?" Lucy exclaims.

"You must remember that we were here when the Wall went up," Oma says softly. "I know what the government can do. I have seen people die trying to cross the border. I have seen the Stasi take good people from their homes—for saying the same things you are."

"Let's not forget what happened to Mr. Schneider next door," says the mother. "He wrote an article for a Western newspaper. It was considered anti-government. He used to be a respected journalist. Now he's in prison."

"What will happen to his family?" Lucy asks.

"That's a good question," says Oma. "Why don't you go next door and bring your friend, Greta, some oranges? Surely her family could use some kindness."

Lucy takes two oranges and walks down the hall. She knocks on the door of the next apartment. *I hope this is it,* she thinks.

"Liesel," says Greta as she peaks out the door. "What are you doing here?"

Lucy holds out the oranges. "My family was sorry to hear what happened to your father," she says.

Greta looks both ways in the hall and opens the door slightly.

"It's good to see you, Liesel," says Greta. "It's been lonely. People are afraid to talk to me in school. Even one of the teachers told the class that my father is a traitor. I look at that wall every night as I try to fall asleep and think that just meters away…"

Greta pauses. "You should go," she says. "I don't want our troubles to become yours."

Lucy leaves the Schneider's apartment. As she walks down the hall, Lucy feels like someone is watching her. All the talk about jail and secret police has made her uneasy.

Lucy opens the door and Hans is waiting for her. "What took you so long?" he asks. "It's time for Hit Parade! Let's bring the radio into my room where Mother can't hear us."

Hans turns on the radio. Lucy knows the song that's playing. She hears it all the time on the 80's radio station that her mother listens to in the car.

"Why would your… I mean Mother, not want us to listen to this?" asks Lucy.

"Where have you been, Liesel?" asks Hans, rolling his eyes. "Between Uncle Kurt and everything else, you know she does not want us listening to radio from the West. It's against the law."

All of a sudden, the door bursts open and a man says, "Hans! Liesel! Change the station!"

"Father, I'm sorry," says Hans with wide eyes. "We were just…"

"I didn't mean to scare you, son," says Hans's father. "But I just heard some rumors on my way home from work. We need to tune into the news."

Before Hans can change the station, a reporter breaks in. "We have just received word that East German citizens will be allowed to cross the border into West Berlin. Travel back and forth will be permitted for people with the proper papers."

Suddenly, Lucy hears people yelling and cheering outside. Horns are honking everywhere. It sounds like the city has come alive.

"We have to cross the border!" cries Lucy. "This is history happening live!"

Oma looks nervous but Lucy guesses she is desperate to see her other son again. The Krugers make a family decision to go to the nearest checkpoint.

"Should we take the car?" asks Mother.

"We were on a waiting list for ten years to get that car!" exclaims Father. "There's no way I'm going to risk losing it to the government."

"We should bring a camera," says Lucy. She can't imagine missing the opportunity to capture these moments.

"I used to take photographs all the time," says Opa. "But I put my camera away years ago. I suppose the guards will have bigger things to worry about tonight."

The family leaves the apartment together and walks toward the nearest checkpoint in a tight group.

As they near the checkpoint, the size of the crowd is shocking. The street is completely filled with people. Many are waving their papers in the air.

"Look," shouts Hans. "They are letting some people cross over."

He hoists Lucy up over his shoulders so she can take a picture. The guards have begun to let a small trickle of people through the gate. Now the crowd is cheering and pressing closer together.

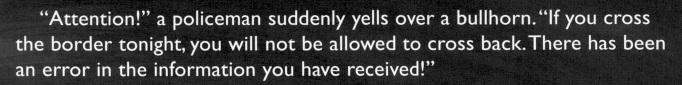

"Attention!" a policeman suddenly yells over a bullhorn. "If you cross the border tonight, you will not be allowed to cross back. There has been an error in the information you have received!"

Lucy feels her heart skip a beat. *What is going on? This isn't the way I thought it happened.*

Lucy knows the Kruger family wants to cross the border, but they are not ready to leave their lives behind. Then Lucy realizes they are not alone. The crowd starts chanting. "Let us cross! We'll come back!"

The people just want the right to travel freely. The threats from the police don't stop the crowd from growing larger.

The Krugers are nearly at the front of the line, when the guards stop to talk to one another. "Don't turn us away now!" Father yells.

Then it happens. The guards open the gate. People flock to them with their papers, but the guards just wave them through. Lucy looks at a guard as she passes. She wonders if he is the one she saw from the apartment window. He gives her a quick smile and flicks his hand as if to say, "Go, now!"

Lucy and the Krugers run through No Man's Land, the gap between the East Berlin checkpoint and the West Berlin checkpoint. Oma grabs Lucy's hand. "Liesel," she yells over the crowd, "we're almost there!"

When they cross the border of West Berlin, Lucy can't believe the scene. Thousands of people are cheering. They are up on rooftops and in the trees. Radios are blaring. News reporters and cameras are everywhere. Lucy pulls out Opa's camera and snaps a picture of people dancing on top of the wall.

"I never thought I'd see this day," Opa says with tears in his eyes.

Lucy and the Kruger family join the celebration. Children hand out candy and flowers to the East Berliners. Hans has a bite of chocolate and says, "This is the best thing I have ever tasted!"

"I can't believe we're here," says Mother.

At that moment, a voice yells, "I knew you would come!" Lucy turns and sees a man who looks just like Liesel's father. She knows it must be Kurt. He runs toward them with his family. In seconds, both families are wrapped up in hugs, kisses and tears.

The reunion is broken up by the sound of metal on concrete. Lucy looks at the Wall. A few men have begun to smash it with sledgehammers. *This is all happening so fast,* she thinks. But then she realizes that it has actually taken twenty-eight years to arrive at this moment. Lucy picks up a tiny chunk of concrete and holds it in her hand.

"This really is a piece of history," she says.

"Of course it's a piece of history, Lucy," Tomas jokes. "We were standing in a history museum last time I checked!"

Maybe you were, Lucy thinks. But then she laughs with her friends. "I guess you're right, Tomas."

"We should really get going," says Emma. "Lucy, you and I have to deal with that cross-town bus on the way home. I don't want to be late for dinner."

"I don't care how long it takes," says Lucy with a smile. "I'm just glad we're free to go wherever we want."

ABOUT THE BERLIN WALL

In 1945, the Nazis surrendered, marking the end of World War II. Berlin, the capital city of Germany, was in ruins. The winners of World War II decided to divide the city into four parts. Each part was run by one of the allied countries: Britain, France, the United States and the Soviet Union.

In 1948, Britain, France and the U.S. introduced a Western German money system and joined their parts of the city. As a result, the Soviets blocked travel to West Berlin.

By 1949, the separation of Germany became official. The Federal Republic of Germany governed the West. It was capitalist and democratic. The German Democratic Republic governed the East. It was a communist dictatorship.

During the 1950s, many East Germans crossed the border into the West. In East Berlin, food and housing were scarce. The people had no say in the government. However, West Berlin was rebuilding at a fast pace. German citizens were in charge of their own government.

Because so many East Germans were leaving, the East German government decided to take action. On August 13, 1961, they began closing the border between East and West Berlin. They put up barbed wire and fences. In a matter of months, a wall 12 feet high and 103 miles long was finished. The military continued to strengthen it for many years.

During the 28 years the Wall stood, many East Germans tried to escape to West Berlin. Hundreds of people died trying to flee. Finally, in August 1989, certain travel restrictions were lifted. Hungary allowed East Germans to travel through their country on their way to Austria and West Germany. Masses of people were also fleeing through Czechoslovakia.

Then on November 9, 1989, it was announced that there would no longer be restrictions on travel in either direction. The announcement was actually made by a government official who had misunderstood the government's new rules. The government was planning to relax travel restrictions, but it had not wanted to lift them altogether. However, East Germans heard the announcement and they showed up at the border to exercise what they thought was their new right to travel. The guards were unprepared and had no choice but to let them through. More than 10,000 East Germans crossed into West Berlin that night. Huge celebrations lasted for days.

Eventually, citizens on both sides of Germany began to break down the Wall. The government did not stop them. In 1990, East Germany reunited with West Germany. They are now one nation, the Federal Republic of Germany.

GLOSSARY

checkpoint: there were eight checkpoints, or border crossings, between East and West Berlin. These allowed visits by West Berliners, other West Germans, western foreigners and Allied personnel into East Berlin. They also allowed rare visits by East German citizens and citizens of other socialist countries into West Berlin, as long as they held the necessary permits.

Cold War: the state of conflict, tension, and competition that existed between the United States (US), a capitalist society, and the Soviet Union (USSR), a communist society, and their allies from the mid-1940s to the early 1990s.

Communism: a political and economic system in which all property is publicly owned. This system is different from capitalism where trade and industry are controlled by the private sector rather than the government.

No Man's Land: a stretch of land between the border posts of East Berlin and West Berlin. The East Berlin checkpoint was actually set inside the border, so the stretch of land still belonged to East Berlin. It was paved with raked gravel, making it easy to spot footprints, and it offered a clear field of fire to the watching armed guards.

Stasi: the East German secret police, which monitored the people and tried to stop any uprising against the government.

GDR: the German Democratic Republic was the socialist/communist government created in the Soviet Zone of occupied Germany.

World War II: a war fought from 1939 to 1945, in which Great Britain, France, the Soviet Union, the United States, China and other allies defeated Germany, Italy and Japan.